Pyramid Fractions, Decimals, & Percents – Fraction Basics Math Workbook

Converting Between Fractions, Decimals, and Percentages (Includes Repeating Decimals)

Chris McMullen, Ph.D.

Pyramid Fractions, Decimals, & Percents – Fraction Basics Math Workbook: Converting Between Fractions, Decimals, and Percentages (Includes Repeating Decimals)

Copyright © 2011 Chris McMullen, Ph.D.

All rights reserved. This includes the right to reproduce any portion of this book in any form. However, teachers who purchase one copy of this book, or borrow one physical copy from a library, may make and distribute photocopies of selected pages for instructional purposes for their own classes only. Also, parents who purchase one copy of this book, or borrow one physical copy from a library, may make and distribute photocopies of selected pages for use by their own children only.

CreateSpace

Nonfiction / Education / Elementary School / Mathematics
Children's / Science / Mathematics / Fractions

ISBN: 1456585924

EAN-13: 978-1456585921

Contents

Introduction	2
Basic Techniques	3
Chapter 1: Converting Fractions to Decimals and Percents	8
Chapter 2: Converting Decimals to Fractions and Percents	15
Chapter 3: Converting Percents to Fractions and Decimals	22
Chapter 4: Converting Fractions to Repeating Decimals	29
Chapter 5: Converting Repeating Decimals to Fractions	36
Answer Key	43

Introduction

These fraction, decimal, and percent problems are presented in a creative visual pattern. The idea behind these pyramid math problems is for the novelty to engage the interest of young students (and perhaps even some teachers and parents, too). In this way, students can improve their math fluency and also enjoy doing the math. This layout also promotes the development of useful visual skills, too.

The answers to all of the problems are tabulated at the back of the book. The first exercise of each part is partially completed and annotated with instructions in order to help students get started. The basic techniques are described on pages 3-7 along with some examples to serve as a guide.

May everyone enjoy pyramid math! ☺

Converting Between Fractions, Decimals, and Percentages (Includes Repeating Decimals)

Basic Techniques

Multiplying Decimals

To multiply numbers with decimals, stack them vertically. Unlike adding and subtracting numbers with decimals, align the **factors** (the two numbers that you are multiplying together) by their rightmost digits (not by the decimal point). Don't worry if the decimal places don't match – as long as the rightmost digits are aligned. Then multiply the numbers the same way that you would multiply whole numbers. Align the intermediate numbers by the rightmost digit the same way that you would ordinarily align them if you were multiplying whole numbers together. Lastly, you need to determine where to put the decimal point in the **product** (that's the final answer). Count the number of digits in each factor that are to the right of their decimal points. Add these two numbers together. Place the decimal point of the product such that the number of digits to the right of its decimal point equals the sum of the numbers of digits to the right of the factors' decimal points. You may need to add leading zeroes to make this possible.

EXAMPLES

$4.23 \times 0.078 =$

$$\begin{array}{r} {}^{1\ 2}\\ {}^{1\ 2}\\ 4.23 \\ \times\ 0.078 \\ \hline 0.03384 \\ 0.29610 \\ \hline 0.32994 \end{array}$$

$0.002 \times 0.5 =$

$$\begin{array}{r} 0.002 \\ \times\ 0.5 \\ \hline 0.0010 \end{array}$$

In the first example, the factor 4.23 has 2 digits to the right of its decimal point and the factor 0.078 has 3 digits to the right of its decimal point. Therefore, the product, 0.32994, has 5 digits to the right of its decimal point. That's how you determine where to put the decimal point in the answer. In the second example, the 0.002 has 3 digits to the right of its decimal point and 0.5 has 1 digit to the right of its decimal point. The answer, 0.0010, must then have 4 digits to the right of its decimal point. Notice that two leading zeroes had to be added (after the decimal point) in order to achieve this. Trailing zeroes of numbers with decimal points may be removed. For example, the answer 0.0010 may also be expressed as 0.001.

Converting Fractions to Decimals

To divide numbers with decimals, arrange them in long division form just as you would if you were dividing whole numbers. Then divide the numbers the same way that you would divide whole numbers. However, instead of writing a remainder, add trailing zeroes to the **dividend** (that's the number you are dividing into) as needed. The decimal position of the **quotient** (the final answer) comes about quite naturally. That is, as you carry out the long division, you multiply digits of the **quotient** (the answer above the dividend) with the **divisor** (that's the number you are dividing by, which appears at the left). You'll have to put the decimal position in the right place (using the rule for multiplying numbers with decimals) in the quotient to make this work.

Study the examples below and refer to them as needed to guide your practice – until you can solve the problems by yourself. When you complete a page of exercises, check your answers in the back of the book – and learn from any mistakes that you might have made.

EXAMPLES

$3/4 = 3 \div 4$

```
   0.75
4) 3.00
   2.80
   0.20
   0.20
      0
```

$12/5 = 12 \div 5$

```
   2.4
5) 12.0
   10.0
    2.0
    2.0
      0
```

$5/8 = 5 \div 8$

```
   0.625
8) 5.000
   4.800
   0.200
    .160
   0.040
   0.040
       0
```

$1/16 = 1 \div 16$

```
    0.0625
16) 1.0000
    0.9600
    0.0400
    0.0320
    0.0080
    0.0080
         0
```

Notice that 3 divided by 4 and 12 divided by 5, for example, would normally be expressed with remainders as 0R1 and 2R2, but by adding the trailing zeros to 3 and 12 to turn them into 3.00 and 12.0, the answers could be expressed as decimals rather than with remainders. In fact, all remainder problems of whole number long division can be expressed in decimal form. For example, 25 divided by 4, which would normally be 6 with a remainder of 1, is found to be 6.25 using the method of long division with decimals. Try it!

Converting Between Fractions, Decimals, and Percentages (Includes Repeating Decimals)

Repeating Decimals

Sometimes, the method of long division with numbers with decimals never ends! That is, you need to keep adding trailing zeroes to the dividend forever. Fortunately, when this happens the digits repeat in a pattern. This is called a **repeating decimal**. For example, 1 divided by 3 results in 0.3333… Try it and see for yourself. The digit 3 repeats forever. This repeating decimal is denoted by adding a bar over it: $0.\overline{3}$. The $\overline{3}$ represents an infinite sequence of 3's. So $0.\overline{3}$ is actually larger than 0.3. Similarly, 11 divided by 9 equals $1.\overline{2}$. Try it yourself.

You might get a repeating sequence of digits rather than a single repeating digit. For example, 20 divided by 11 equals $1.\overline{81}$. Try it and see. In this case, the 81 sequence repeats over and over. That is, $1.\overline{81}$ represents 1.818181… The 81 repeats forever. The sequence may be long. For example, 3 divided by 7 equals $0.\overline{428571}$.

Study the examples below and refer to them as needed to guide your practice – until you can solve the problems by yourself. When you complete a page of exercises, check your answers in the back of the book – and learn from any mistakes that you might have made.

EXAMPLES

$0.337 \div 1.8$

$0.05 \div 0.6$

$$0.08\overline{3}$$
$$0.6\overline{)0.0500}$$
$$\underline{0.048}$$
$$0.0020$$
$$\underline{0.0018}$$
$$0.00020$$

$$0.187\overline{2}$$
$$1.8\overline{)0.337}$$
$$\underline{0.18}$$
$$0.157$$
$$\underline{0.144}$$
$$0.0130$$
$$\underline{0.0126}$$
$$0.00040$$
$$\underline{0.00036}$$
$$0.000040$$

Notice that the 20 and 40 repeat at the end of these examples. This is how you know if and when the decimal is repeating.

Converting Nonrepeating Decimals to Fractions

A nonrepeating decimal can be converted to a fraction as follows: (1) Figure out what power of ten you need to multiply the decimal by in order to remove the decimal point. Here are some examples: Multiply 0.4 by 10 to make 4, multiply 0.12 by 100 to make 12, and multiply 0.375 by 1000 to make 375. (2) Use the number without a decimal point as the numerator and use the power of 10 from Step 1 as the denominator. For the examples above, you would get 4/10, 12/100, and 375/1000. (3) If the resulting fraction is reducible, cancel the greatest common factor to reduce it. For the examples above, 4/10 becomes 2/5 by dividing numerator and denominator by 2, 12/100 becomes 3/25 by canceling the greatest common factor of 4, and 375/1000 becomes 3/8 by dividing through by 125.

EXAMPLES

$0.25 = 25/100 = 1/4$, $1.5 = 15/10 = 3/2$, $0.004 = 4/1000 = 1/250$

Converting Repeating Decimals to Fractions

A repeating decimal can be converted to a fraction as follows: (1) Multiply by the power of 10 needed so that the repeating digits will disappear if the original repeating decimal is subtracted from the new number. As examples, multiply $0.\overline{3}$ by 10 to make $3.\overline{3}$, multiply $0.4\overline{1}$ by 10 to make $4.\overline{1}$, and multiply $.0\overline{300}$ by 1000 to make $30.\overline{03}$. When you multiply by the power of 10, remember that the overbar represents a sequence of digits that repeats forever. (2) Subtract the original repeating decimal from the new one (that you obtained in Step 1 by multiplying by a power of 10). This subtraction cancels the repeating decimal. Use this as the numerator. Subtract 1 from the power of 10 and use that as the denominator. In the above examples, you would get 3/9, 3.7/9, and 30/999. (3) If the numerator is a decimal, multiply both the numerator and denominator by the power of 10 needed to make the numerator an integer. (4) If the resulting fraction is reducible, cancel the greatest common factor to reduce it. For the examples above, 3/9 becomes 1/3, 37/90 is irreducible, and 30/999 becomes 10/333.

EXAMPLES

$0.\overline{6} = (6.\overline{6} - 0.\overline{6})/9 = 6/9 = 2/3$, $0.\overline{45} = (45.\overline{45} - 0.\overline{45})/99 = 45/99 = 5/11$

$1.\overline{7} = (17.\overline{7} - 1.\overline{7})/9 = 16/9$, $0.\overline{148} = (148.\overline{148} - 0.\overline{148})/999 = 148/999 = 4/27$

$4.\overline{3} = (43.\overline{3} - 4.\overline{3})/9 = 39/9 = 13/3$, $1.4\overline{7} = (14.\overline{7} - 1.4\overline{7})/9 = 13.3/9 = 133/90$

$0.0\overline{58} = (5.8\overline{58} - 0.0\overline{58})/99 = 5.8/99 = 58/990 = 29/495$

Converting Between Fractions, Decimals, and Percentages (Includes Repeating Decimals)

Relating Percentages to Fractions and Decimals

To convert a decimal to a percentage, simply multiply by 100 and add a % sign to the end of the number. To convert a percentage to a decimal, do just the opposite: That is, divide by 100 and remove the % sign.

EXAMPLES

$0.42 = 0.42 \times 100\% = 42\%$, $1.3 = 1.3 \times 100\% = 130\%$, $0.1 = 0.1 \times 100\% = 10\%$

$75\% = 75/100 = 0.75$, $250\% = 250/100 = 2.5$, $0.8\% = 0.8/100 = 0.008$

To convert a percentage to a fraction, first convert the percentage to a decimal and then convert the decimal to a fraction. Similarly, to convert a fraction to a percentage, first change it to decimal form and then make the percentage.

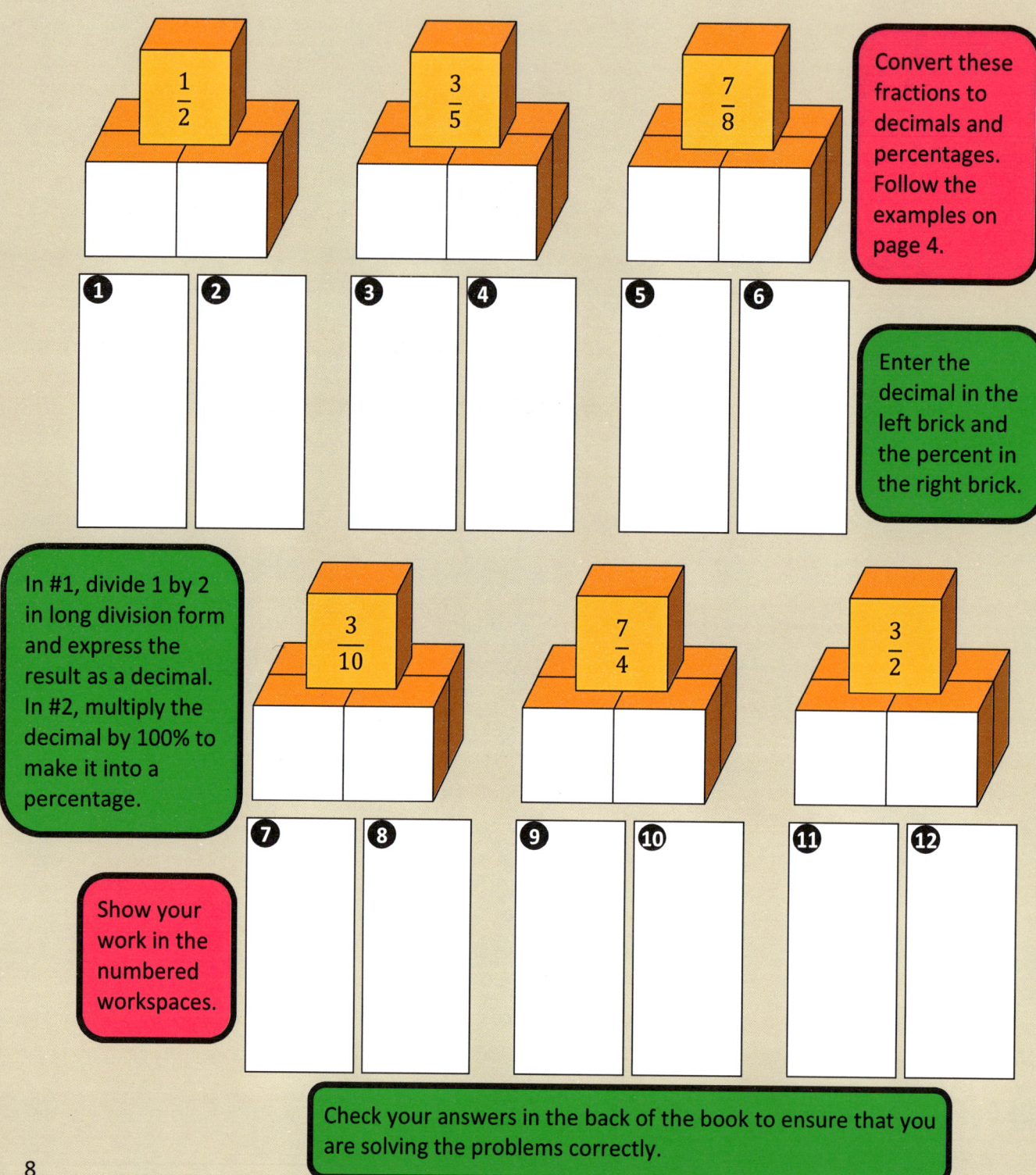

Converting Between Fractions, Decimals, and Percentages (Includes Repeating Decimals)

Pyramid Fractions, Decimals, & Percents – Fraction Basics Math Workbook

Converting Between Fractions, Decimals, and Percentages (Includes Repeating Decimals)

Pyramid Fractions, Decimals, & Percents – Fraction Basics Math Workbook

Converting Between Fractions, Decimals, and Percentages (Includes Repeating Decimals)

Pyramid Fractions, Decimals, & Percents – Fraction Basics Math Workbook

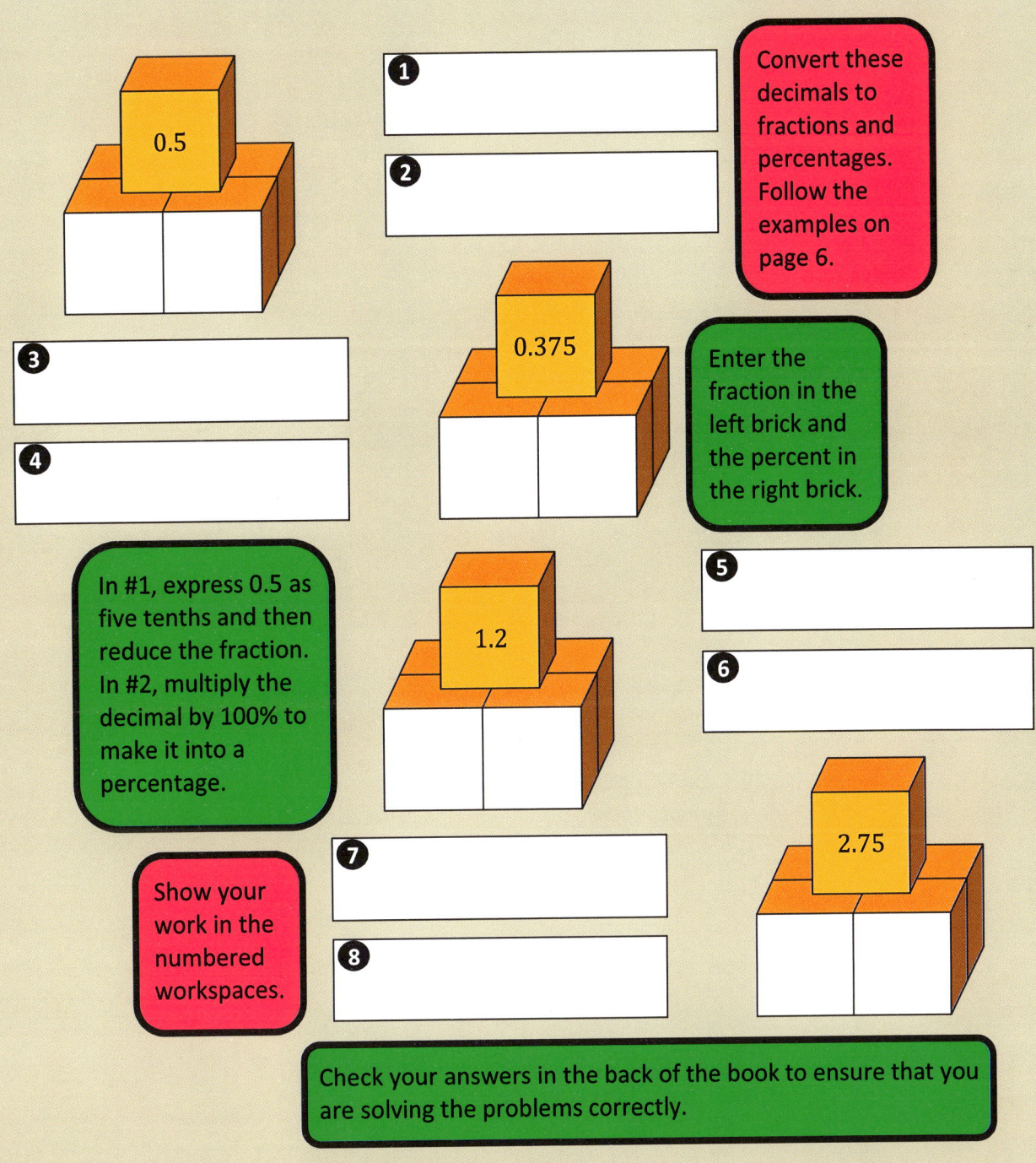

Pyramid Fractions, Decimals, & Percents – Fraction Basics Math Workbook

Converting Between Fractions, Decimals, and Percentages (Includes Repeating Decimals)

Pyramid Fractions, Decimals, & Percents – Fraction Basics Math Workbook

Converting Between Fractions, Decimals, and Percentages (Includes Repeating Decimals)

Pyramid Fractions, Decimals, & Percents – Fraction Basics Math Workbook

Converting Between Fractions, Decimals, and Percentages (Includes Repeating Decimals)

3 Converting Percents to Fractions and Decimals

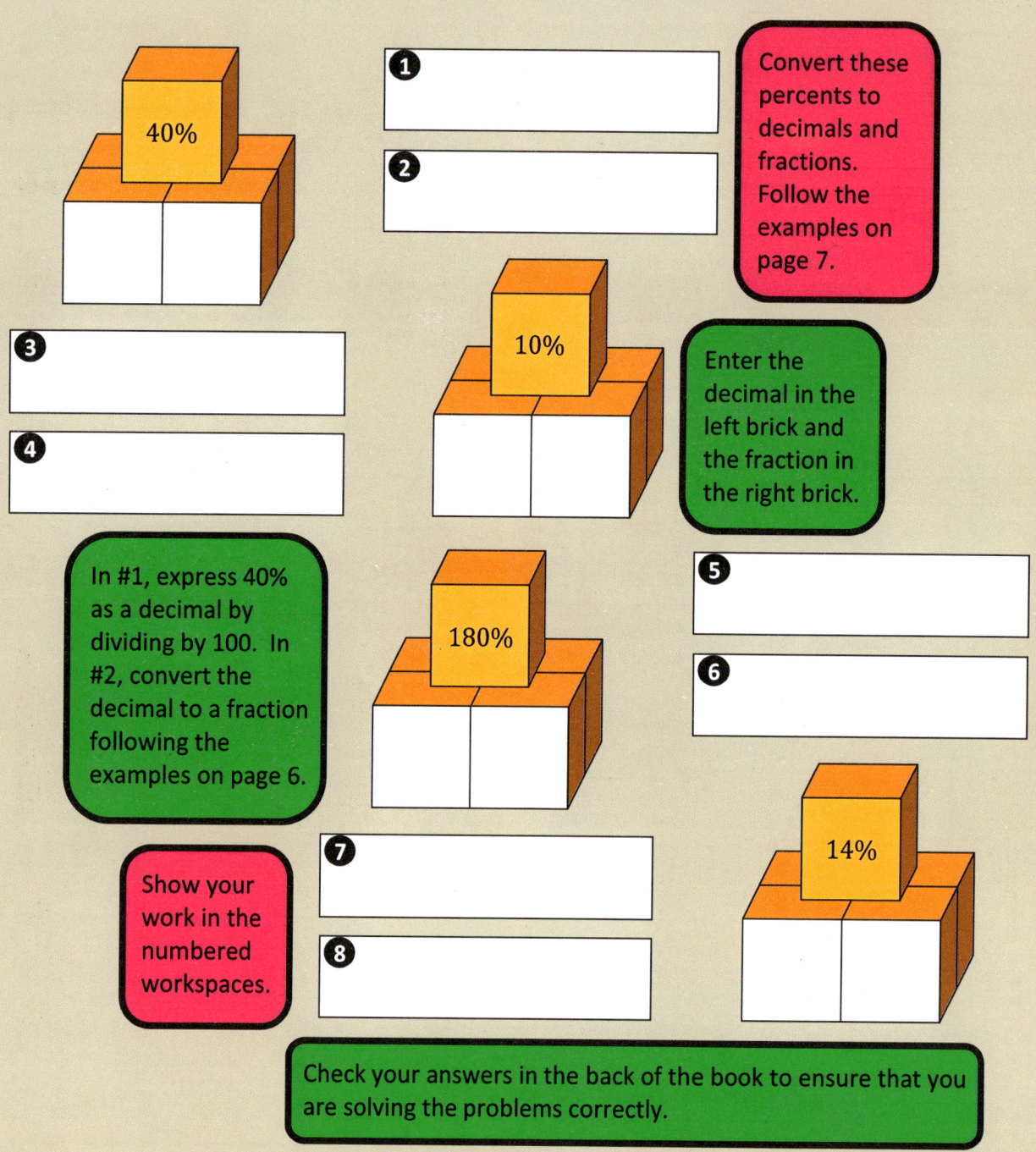

Converting Between Fractions, Decimals, and Percentages (Includes Repeating Decimals)

Pyramid Fractions, Decimals, & Percents – Fraction Basics Math Workbook

Converting Between Fractions, Decimals, and Percentages (Includes Repeating Decimals)

Pyramid Fractions, Decimals, & Percents – Fraction Basics Math Workbook

Converting Between Fractions, Decimals, and Percentages (Includes Repeating Decimals)

Pyramid Fractions, Decimals, & Percents – Fraction Basics Math Workbook

Converting Between Fractions, Decimals, and Percentages (Includes Repeating Decimals)

4 Converting Fractions to Repeating Decimals

WORKSPACE

Convert these fractions to repeating decimals and percentages. Follow the examples on page 5.

Enter the decimal in the left brick and the percent in the right brick.

Check your answers in the back of the book to ensure that you are solving the problems correctly.

Show your work in the workspace above.

Pyramid Fractions, Decimals, & Percents – Fraction Basics Math Workbook

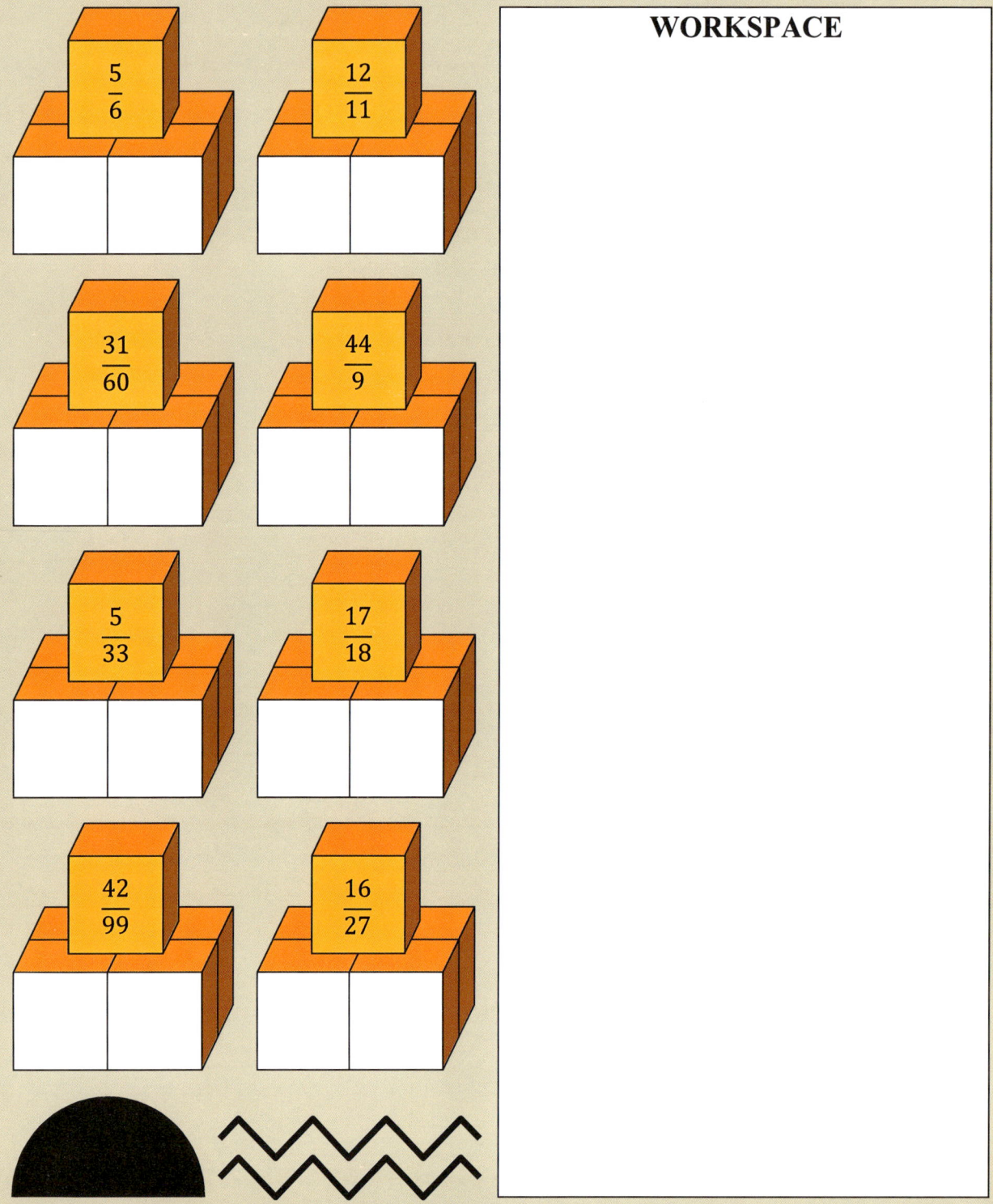

Converting Between Fractions, Decimals, and Percentages (Includes Repeating Decimals)

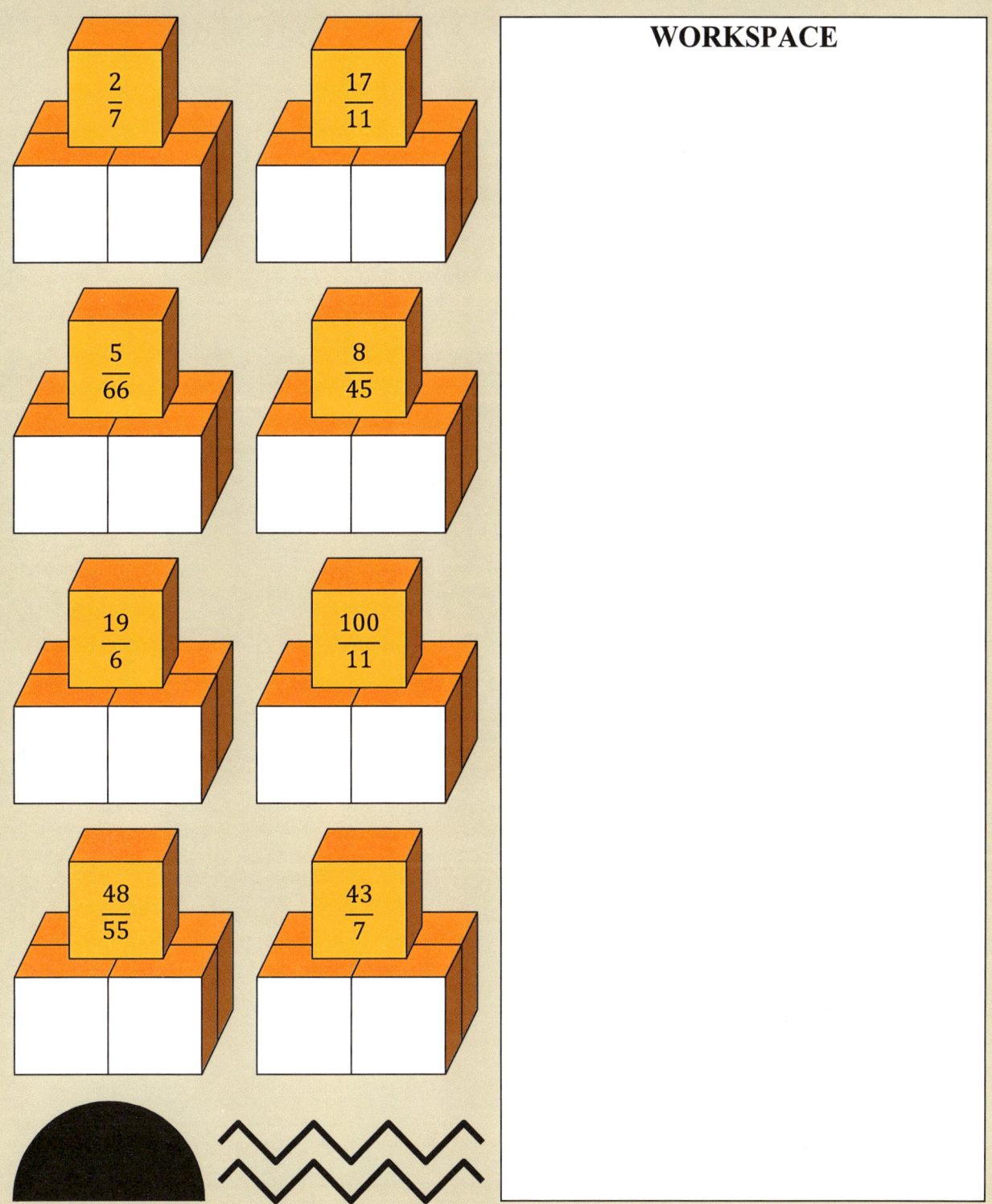

Pyramid Fractions, Decimals, & Percents – Fraction Basics Math Workbook

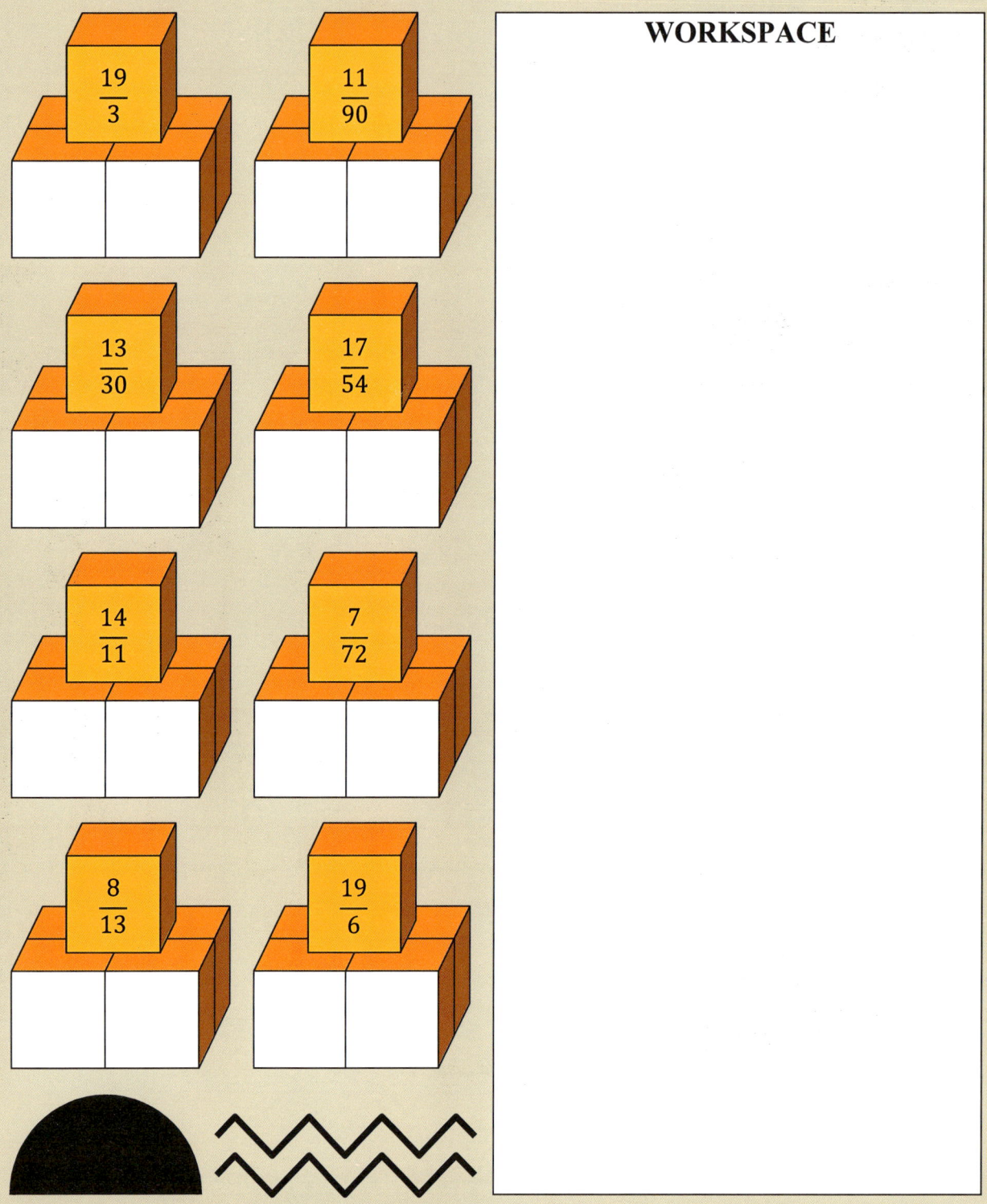

32

Converting Between Fractions, Decimals, and Percentages (Includes Repeating Decimals)

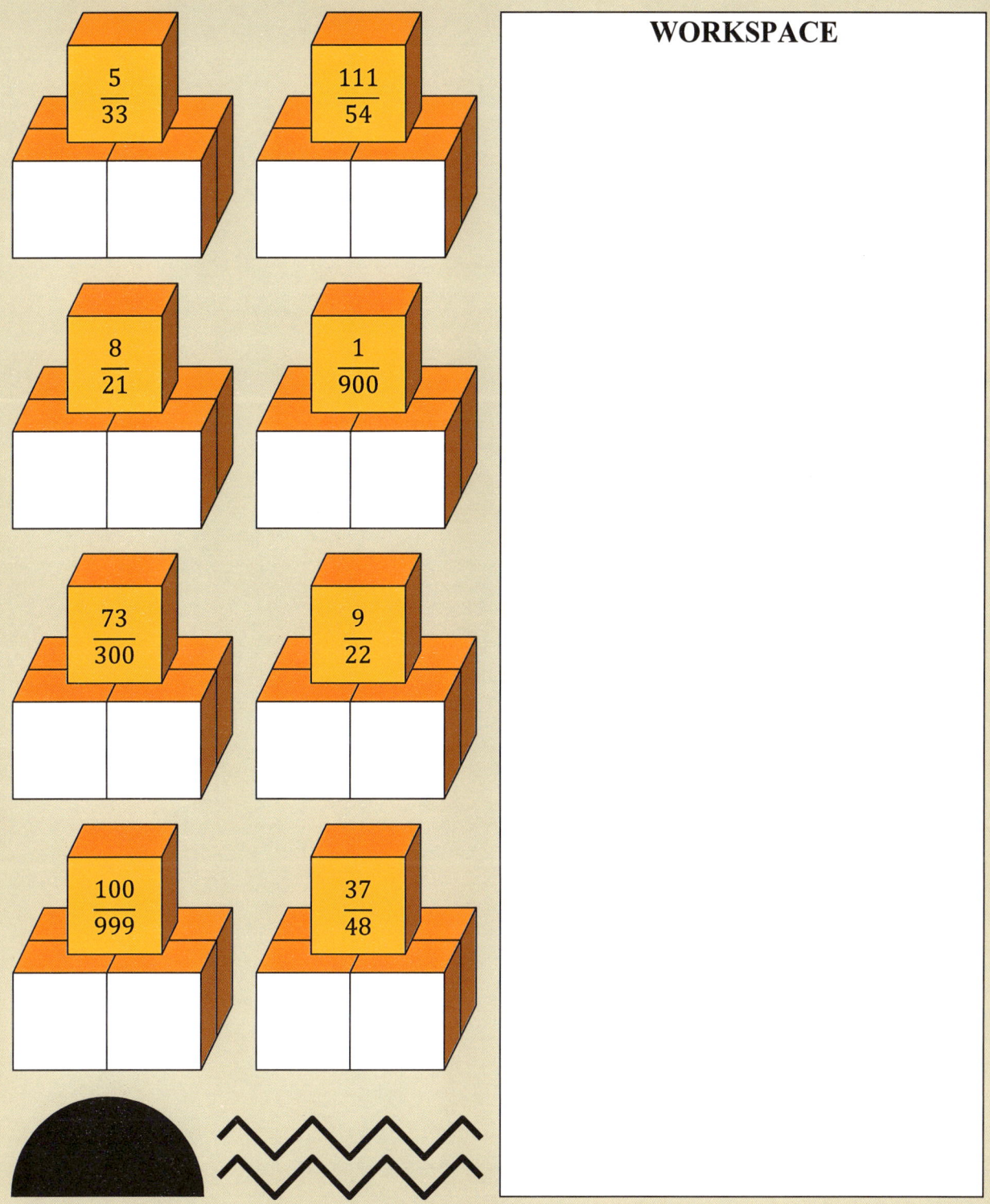

Pyramid Fractions, Decimals, & Percents – Fraction Basics Math Workbook

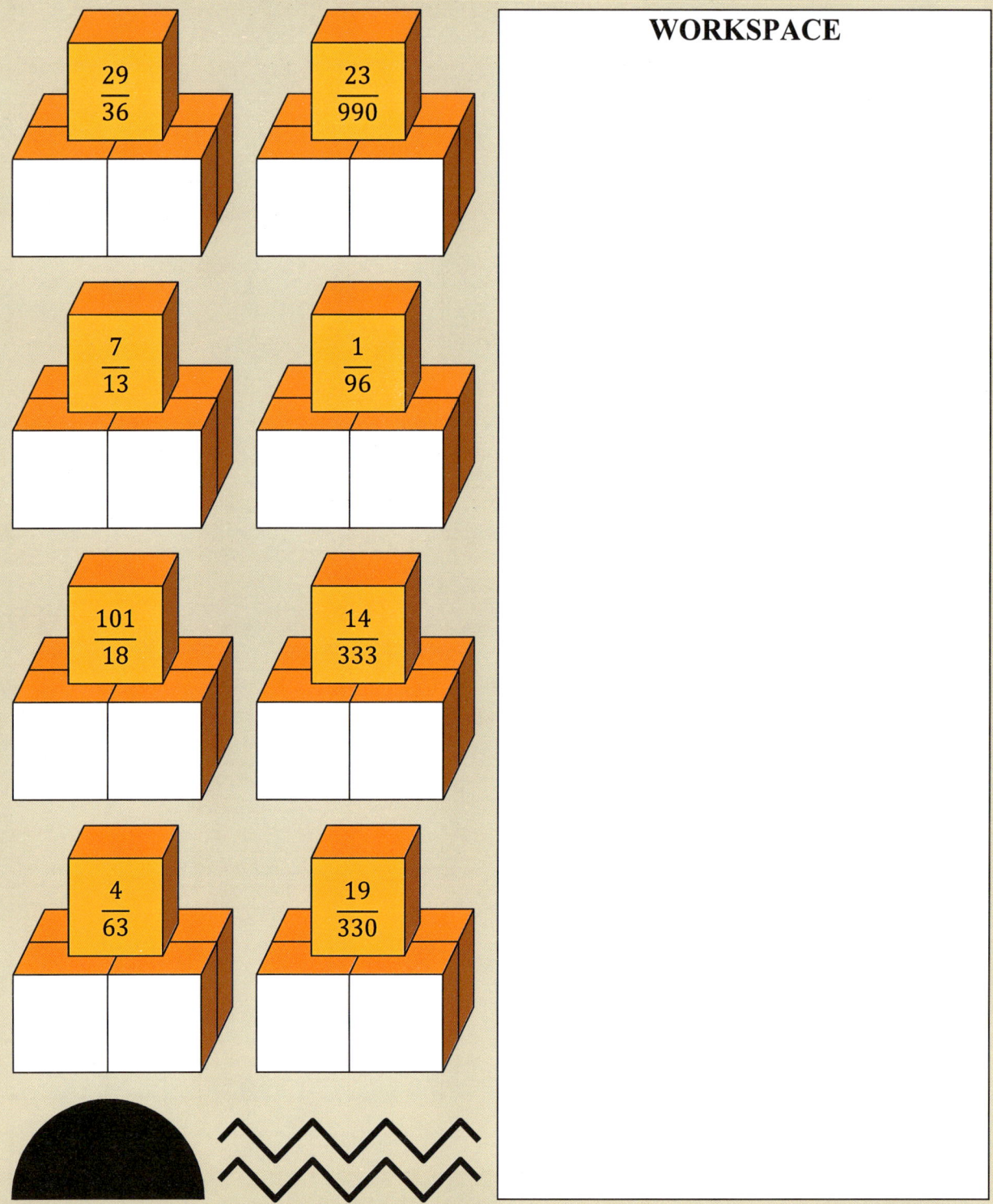

Converting Between Fractions, Decimals, and Percentages (Includes Repeating Decimals)

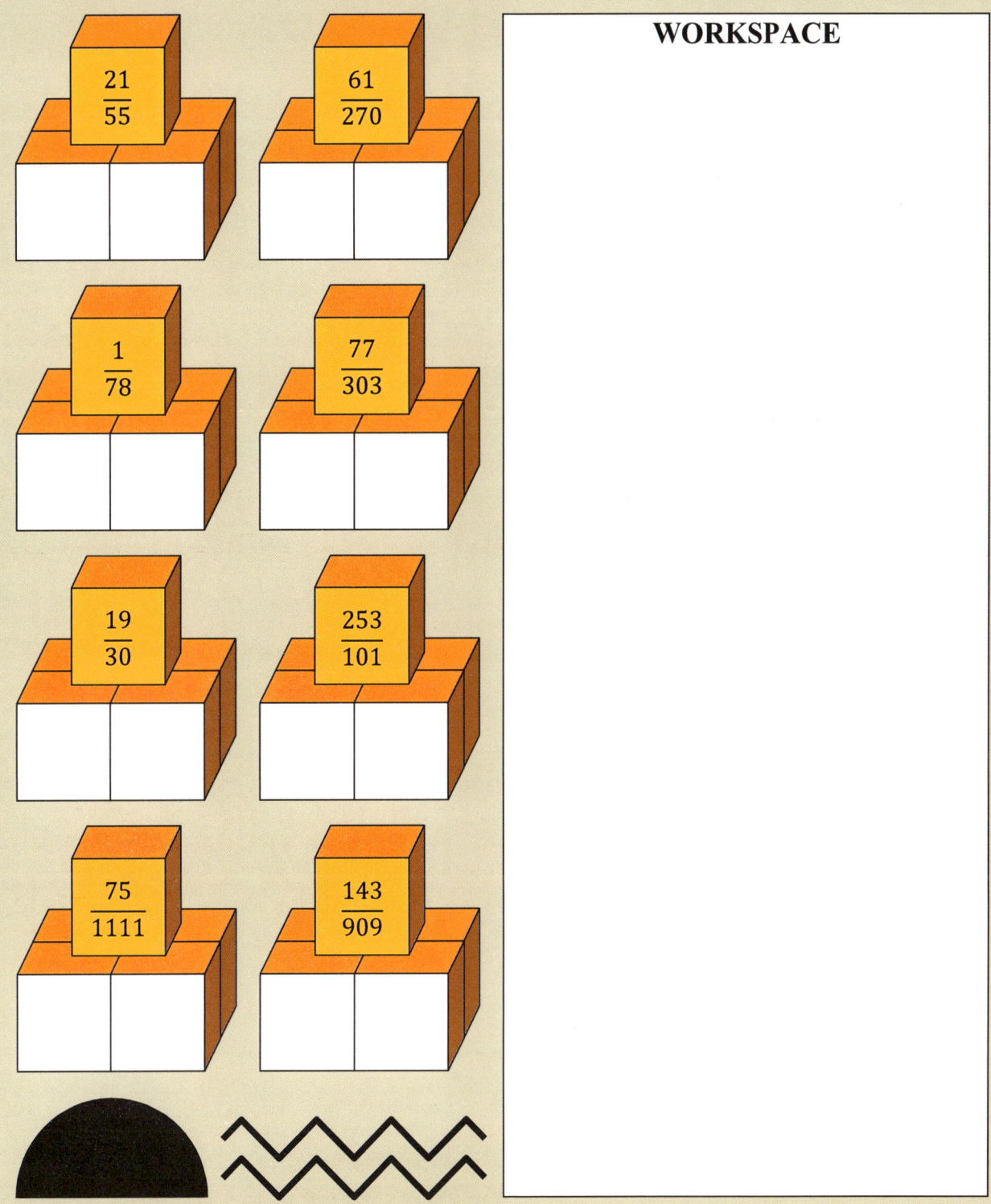

WORKSPACE

Pyramid Fractions, Decimals, & Percents – Fraction Basics Math Workbook

5 Converting Repeating Decimals to Fractions

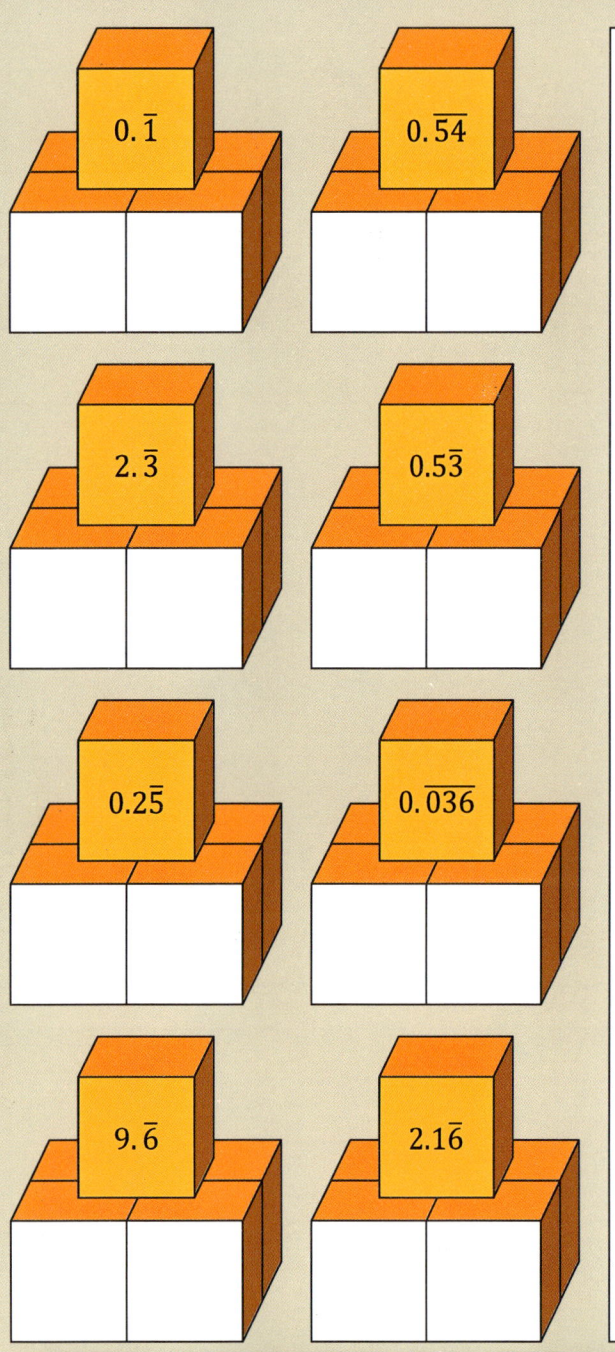

WORKSPACE

Convert these repeating decimals to fractions and percentages. Follow the examples on pages 6-7.

Enter the fraction in the left brick and the percent in the right brick.

Check your answers in the back of the book to ensure that you are solving the problems correctly.

Show your work in the workspace above.

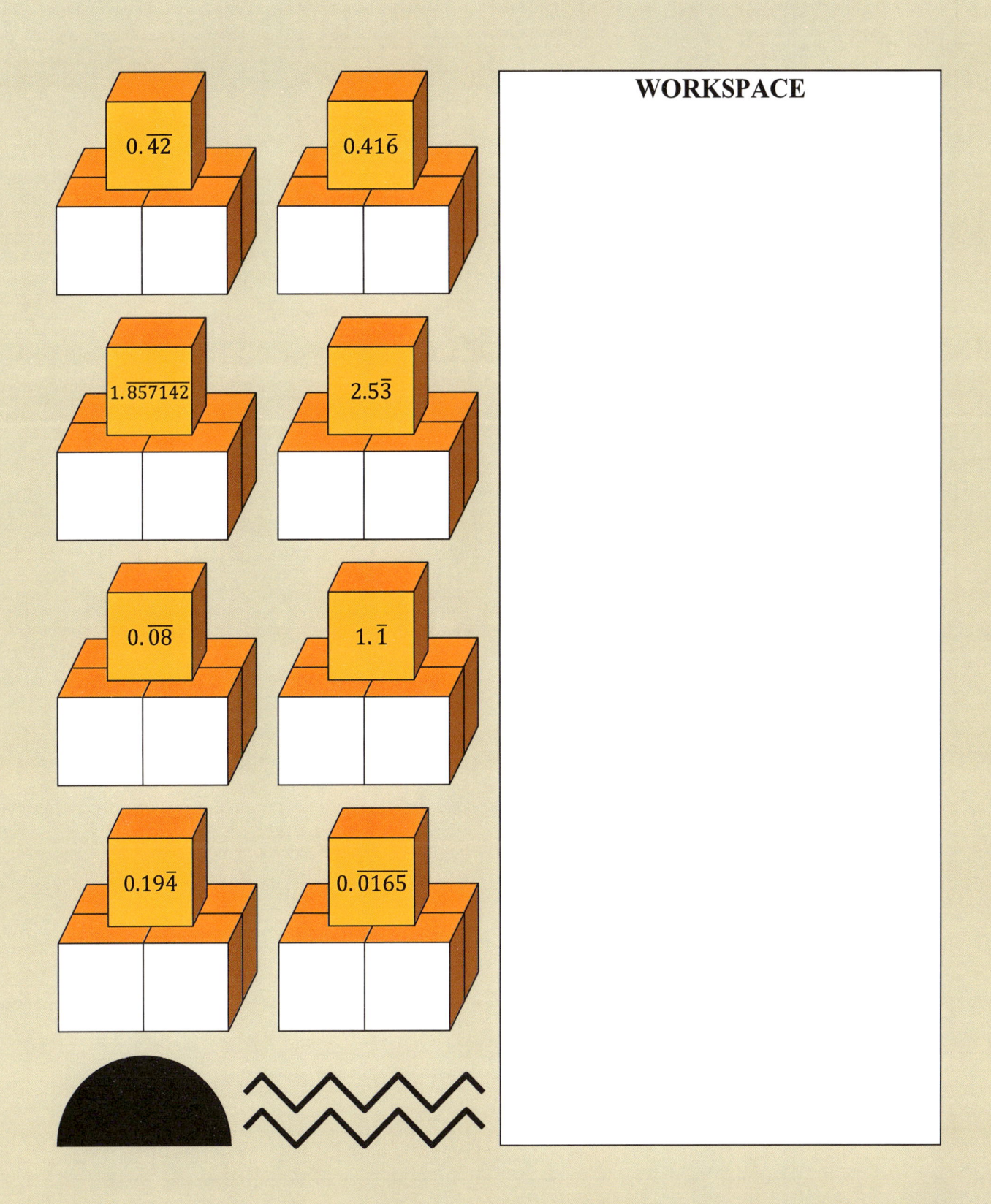

Converting Between Fractions, Decimals, and Percentages (Includes Repeating Decimals)

$0.\overline{42}$

$0.41\overline{6}$

$1.85714\overline{2}$

$2.5\overline{3}$

$0.\overline{08}$

$1.\overline{1}$

$0.19\overline{4}$

$0.\overline{0165}$

WORKSPACE

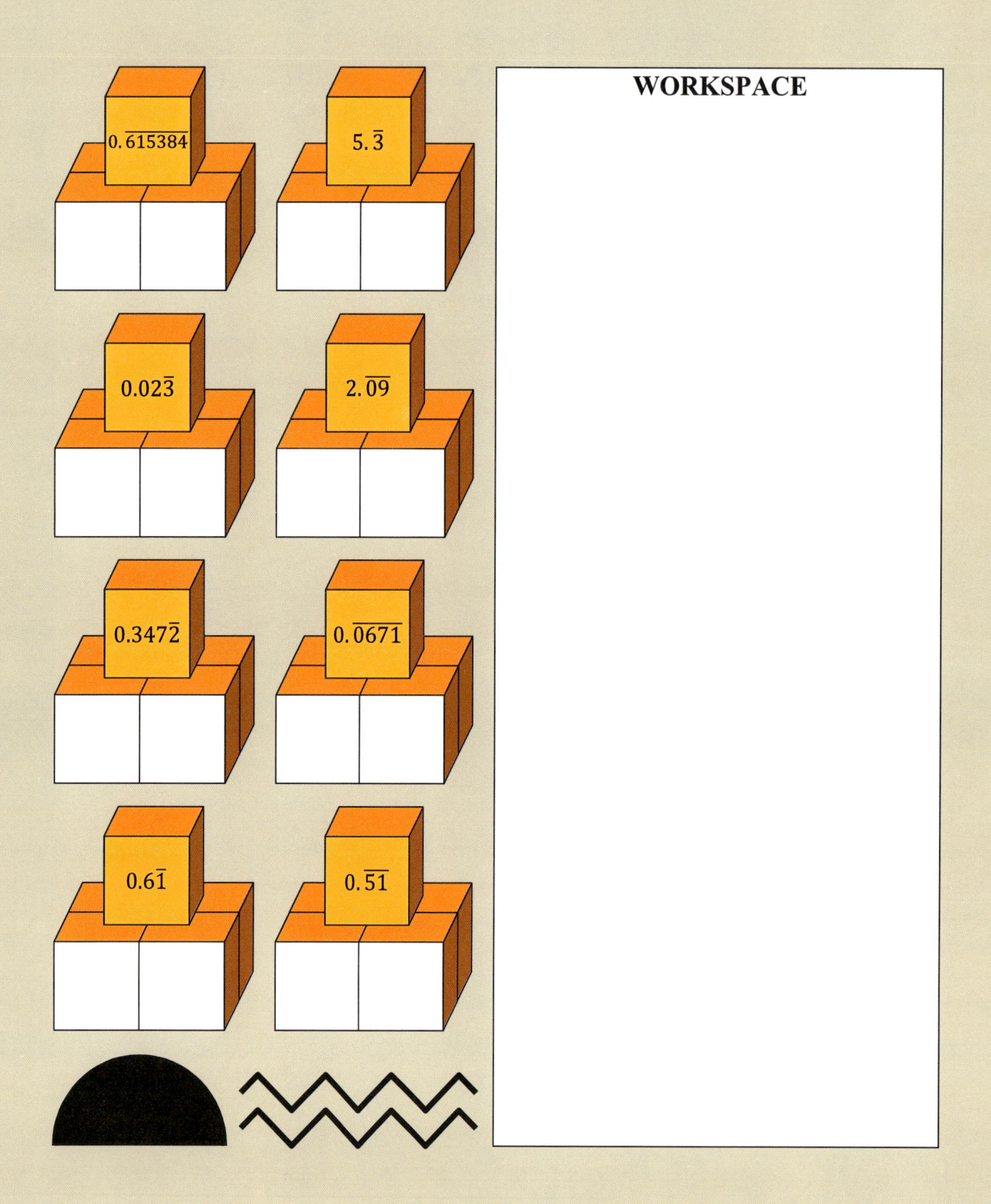

Pyramid Fractions, Decimals, & Percents – Fraction Basics Math Workbook

$0.\overline{615384}$

$5.\overline{3}$

$0.02\overline{3}$

$2.\overline{09}$

$0.347\overline{2}$

$0.\overline{0671}$

$0.6\overline{1}$

$0.\overline{51}$

WORKSPACE

38

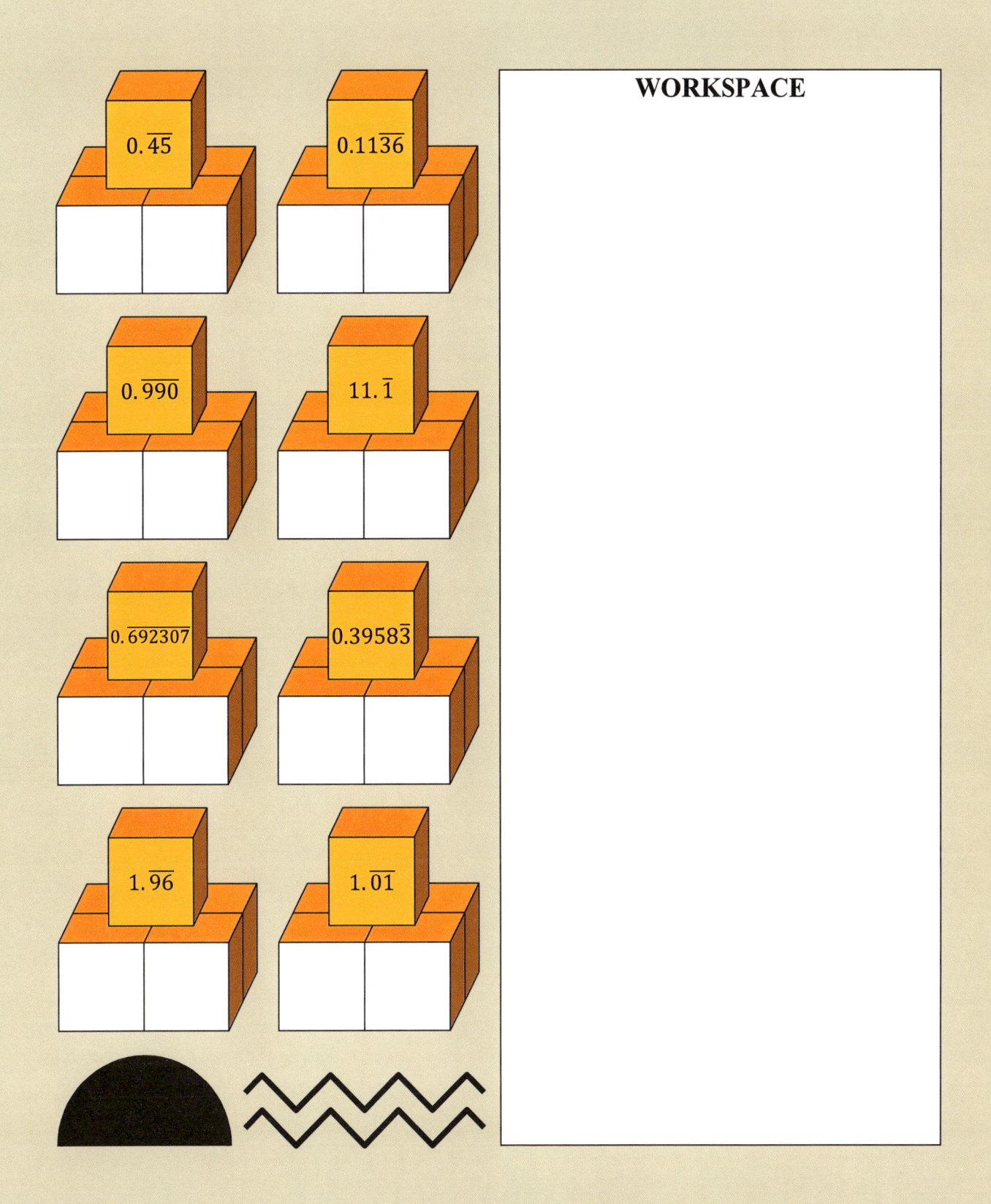

Converting Between Fractions, Decimals, and Percentages (Includes Repeating Decimals)

$0.\overline{45}$

$0.11\overline{36}$

$0.\overline{990}$

$11.\overline{1}$

$0.\overline{692307}$

$0.3958\overline{3}$

$1.\overline{96}$

$1.\overline{01}$

WORKSPACE

39

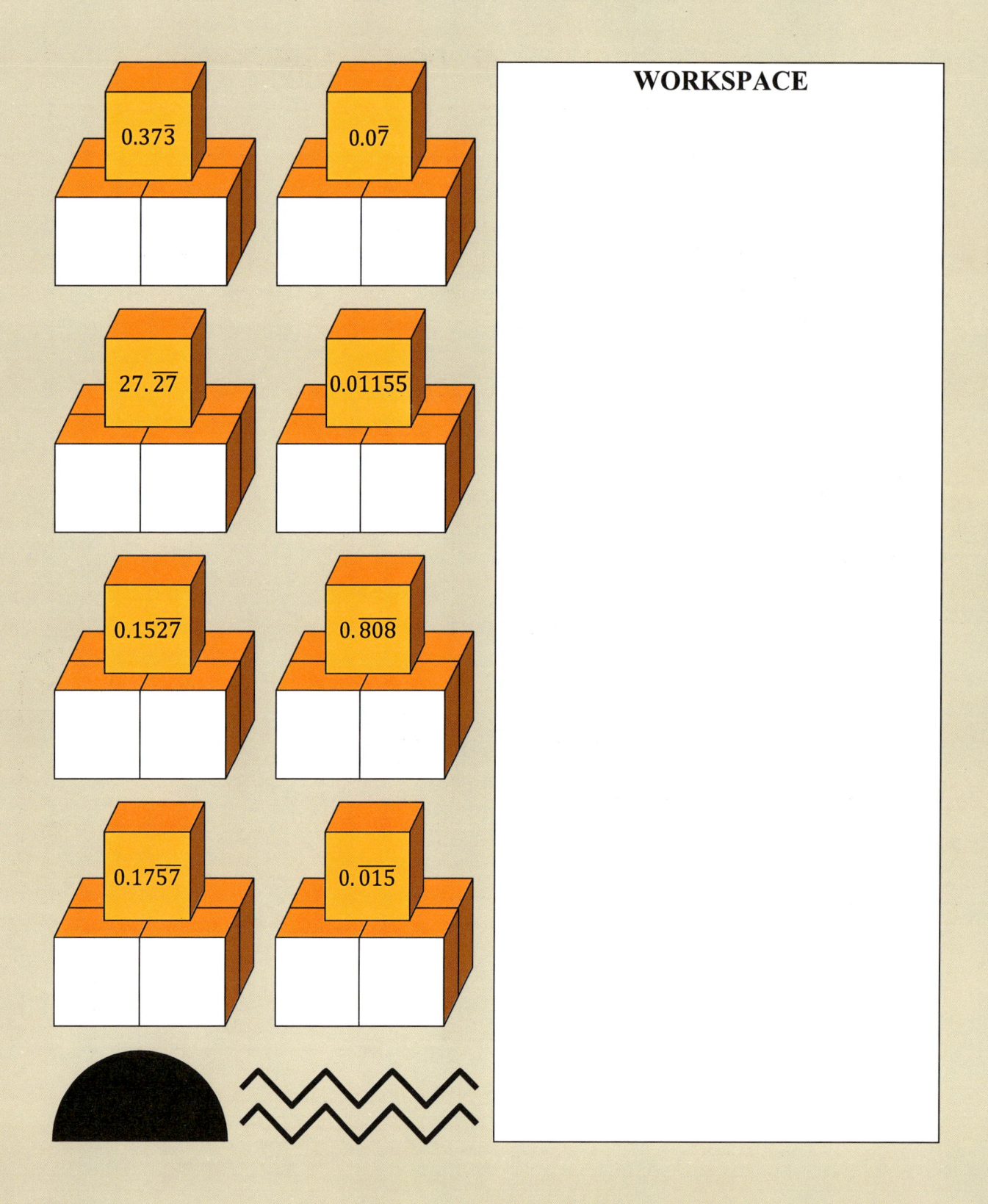

Pyramid Fractions, Decimals, & Percents – Fraction Basics Math Workbook

$0.37\overline{3}$

$0.0\overline{7}$

$27.\overline{27}$

$0.0\overline{1155}$

$0.15\overline{27}$

$0.\overline{808}$

$0.17\overline{57}$

$0.\overline{015}$

WORKSPACE

40

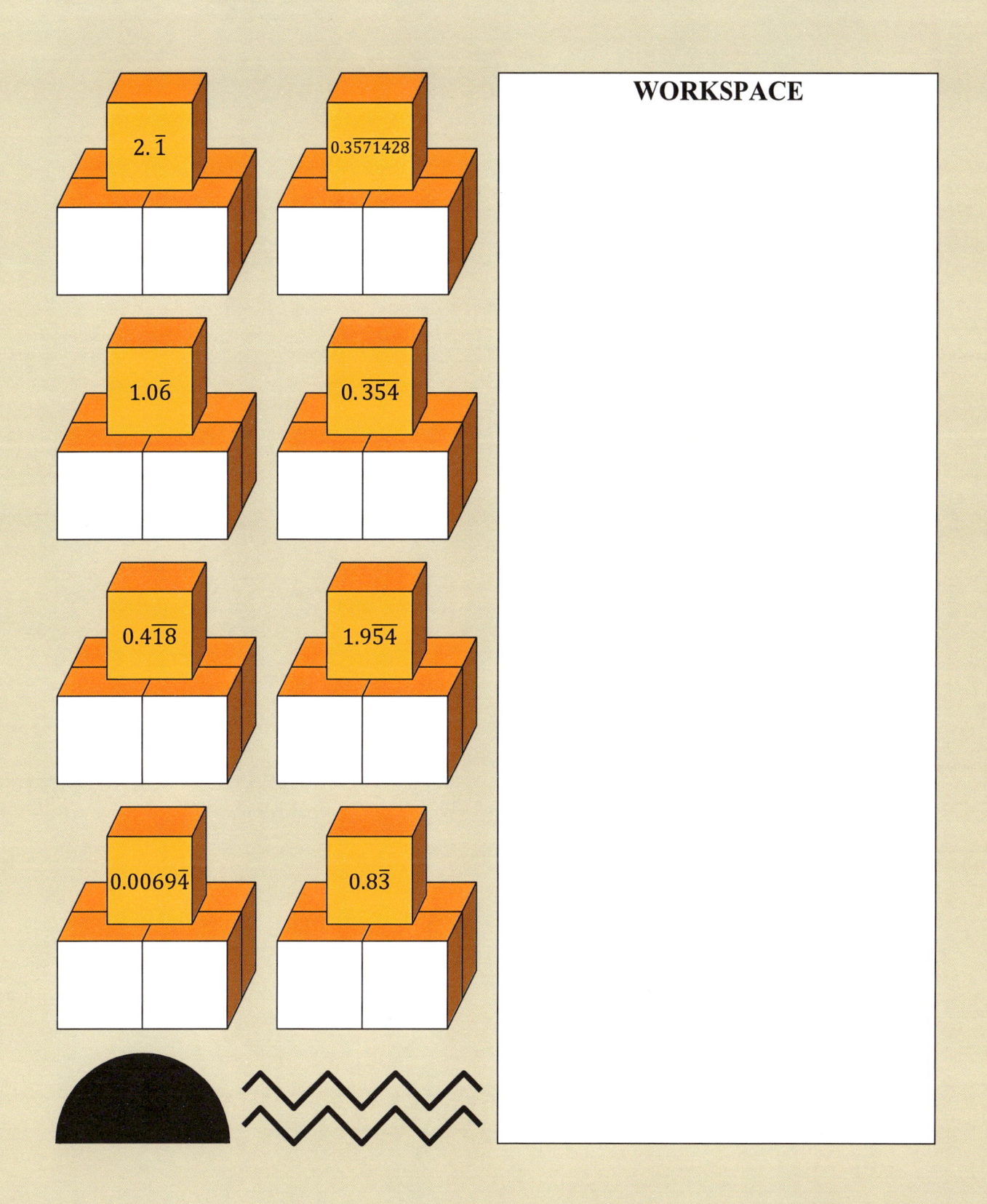

Converting Between Fractions, Decimals, and Percentages (Includes Repeating Decimals)

- $2.\overline{1}$
- $0.3\overline{571428}$
- $1.0\overline{6}$
- $0.\overline{354}$
- $0.4\overline{18}$
- $1.9\overline{54}$
- $0.0069\overline{4}$
- $0.8\overline{3}$

WORKSPACE

Pyramid Fractions, Decimals, & Percents – Fraction Basics Math Workbook

$0.9\overline{4}$

$0.50\overline{25}$

$0.\overline{703}$

$0.0208\overline{3}$

$0.170\overline{45}$

$0.97\overline{2}$

$0.\overline{476190}$

$2.98\overline{14}$

WORKSPACE

42

Converting Between Fractions, Decimals, and Percentages (Includes Repeating Decimals)

Answer Key

			Answer Key			
Page 8	0.5	0.6	0.875	0.3	1.75	1.5
	50%	60%	87.5%	30%	175%	150%
Page 9	0.3125	0.16	0.11	2.25	5.5	1.6
	31.25%	16%	11%	225%	550%	160%
Page 10	0.42	1.375	0.28125	0.041	5.4	0.25
	42%	137.5%	28.125%	4.1%	540%	25%
Page 11	0.125	0.52	0.9375	3.5	2.9	0.164
	12.5%	52%	93.75%	350%	290%	16.4%
Page 12	0.072	0.1875	1.68	2.125	0.8	0.234375
	7.2%	18.75%	168%	212.5%	80%	23.4375%
Page 13	4.4	12.1	0.007	2.5	0.4	0.01
	440%	1210%	0.7%	250%	40%	1%
Page 14	0.34375	1.52	0.015625	0.006	3.125	0.18
	34.375%	152%	1.5625%	0.6%	312.5%	18%
Page 15	1/2	3/8	6/5	11/4		
	50%	37.5%	120%	275%		
Page 16	1/5	3/4	13/10	7/20	31/25	
	20%	75%	130%	35%	124%	
Page 17	2/25	5/8	9/50	12/5	19/20	
	8%	62.5%	18%	240%	95%	
Page 18	3/8	17/10	1/50	26/25	18/125	
	37.5%	170%	2%	104%	14.4%	
Page 19	8/5	9/2	36/25	3/250	11/4	
	160%	450%	144%	1.2%	275%	
Page 20	33/40	1/1000	24/25	287/250	9/25	
	82.5%	0.1%	96%	114.8%	36%	
Page 21	41/50	9/16	13/4	21/50	187/100	
	82%	56.25%	325%	42%	187%	
Page 22	2/5	1/10	9/5	7/50		
	0.4	0.1	1.8	0.14		
Page 23	3/4	3/2	12/25	3/50	7/25	
	0.75	1.5	0.48	0.06	0.28	
Page 24	1/200	5/8	1/25	6/5	31/100	
	0.005	0.625	0.04	1.2	0.31	
Page 25	7/2	1/125	9/40	7/20	27/200	
	3.5	0.008	0.225	0.35	0.135	
Page 26	17/20	111/250	9/125	11/4	6/25	
	0.85	0.444	0.072	2.75	0.24	
Page 27	12/125	14/25	9/8	1/40	3/5	
	0.096	0.56	1.125	0.025	0.6	
Page 28	1/50	6/5	7/16	1/125	13/100	
	0.02	1.2	0.4375	0.008	0.13	

43

Pyramid Fractions, Decimals, & Percents – Fraction Basics Math Workbook

Page 29	$0.\overline{6}$	$0.\overline{4}$	$1.\overline{6}$	$0.\overline{45}$	$0.5\overline{3}$	$0.3\overline{18}$	$0.41\overline{6}$	$1.8\overline{3}$
	$66.\overline{6}\%$	$44.\overline{4}\%$	$166.\overline{6}\%$	$45.\overline{45}\%$	$53.\overline{3}\%$	$31.\overline{81}\%$	$41.\overline{6}\%$	$183.\overline{3}\%$
Page 30	$0.8\overline{3}$	$1.\overline{09}$	$0.51\overline{6}$	$4.\overline{8}$	$0.\overline{15}$	$0.9\overline{4}$	$0.\overline{42}$	$0.\overline{592}$
	$83.\overline{3}\%$	$109.\overline{09}\%$	$51.\overline{6}\%$	$488.\overline{8}\%$	$15.\overline{15}\%$	$94.\overline{4}\%$	$42.\overline{42}\%$	$59.\overline{259}\%$
Page 31	$0.\overline{285714}$	$1.\overline{54}$	$0.0\overline{75}$	$0.1\overline{7}$	$3.1\overline{6}$	$9.\overline{09}$	$0.8\overline{72}$	$6.\overline{142857}$
	$28.\overline{571428}\%$	$154.\overline{54}\%$	$7.\overline{57}\%$	$17.\overline{7}\%$	$316.\overline{6}\%$	$909.\overline{09}\%$	$87.\overline{27}\%$	$614.\overline{285714}\%$
Page 32	$6.\overline{3}$	$0.1\overline{2}$	$0.4\overline{3}$	$0.3\overline{148}$	$1.\overline{27}$	$0.097\overline{2}$	$0.\overline{615384}$	$3.1\overline{6}$
	$633.\overline{3}\%$	$12.\overline{2}\%$	$43.\overline{3}\%$	$31.\overline{481}\%$	$127.\overline{27}\%$	$9.7\overline{2}\%$	$61.\overline{538461}\%$	$316.\overline{6}\%$
Page 33	$0.\overline{15}$	$2.0\overline{5}$	$0.\overline{380952}$	$0.00\overline{1}$	$0.24\overline{3}$	$0.4\overline{09}$	$0.\overline{100}$	$0.770\overline{83}$
	$15.\overline{15}\%$	$205.\overline{5}\%$	$38.\overline{095238}\%$	$0.\overline{1}\%$	$24.\overline{3}\%$	$40.\overline{90}\%$	$10.\overline{010}\%$	$77.08\overline{3}\%$
Page 34	$0.80\overline{5}$	$0.0\overline{23}$	$0.\overline{538461}$	$0.0104\overline{16}$	$5.6\overline{1}$	$0.\overline{042}$	$0.0\overline{634920}$	$0.05\overline{7}$
	$80.\overline{5}\%$	$2.\overline{32}\%$	$53.\overline{846153}\%$	$1.041\overline{6}\%$	$561.\overline{1}\%$	$4.\overline{204}\%$	$6.\overline{349206}\%$	$5.7\overline{5}\%$
Page 35	$0.38\overline{1}$	$0.2\overline{259}$	$0.0\overline{128205}$	$0.\overline{2541}$	$0.6\overline{3}$	$2.\overline{5049}$	$0.0\overline{675}$	$0.\overline{1573}$
	$38.\overline{18}\%$	$22.\overline{592}\%$	$1.\overline{282051}\%$	$25.\overline{4125}\%$	$63.\overline{3}\%$	$250.\overline{4950}\%$	$6.7\overline{506}\%$	$15.\overline{7315}\%$
Page 36	$\dfrac{1}{9}$	$\dfrac{6}{11}$	$\dfrac{7}{3}$	$\dfrac{8}{15}$	$\dfrac{23}{90}$	$\dfrac{4}{111}$	$\dfrac{87}{9}$	$\dfrac{13}{6}$
	$11.\overline{1}\%$	$54.\overline{54}\%$	$233.\overline{3}\%$	$53.\overline{3}\%$	$25.5\overline{5}\%$	$3.\overline{603}\%$	$966.\overline{6}\%$	$216.\overline{6}\%$
Page 37	$\dfrac{14}{33}$	$\dfrac{5}{12}$	$\dfrac{13}{7}$	$\dfrac{38}{15}$	$\dfrac{8}{99}$	$\dfrac{10}{9}$	$\dfrac{7}{36}$	$\dfrac{5}{303}$
	$42.\overline{42}\%$	$41.\overline{6}\%$	$185.\overline{714285}\%$	$253.\overline{3}\%$	$8.\overline{08}\%$	$111.\overline{1}\%$	$19.\overline{4}\%$	$1.\overline{6501}\%$
Page 38	$\dfrac{8}{13}$	$\dfrac{16}{3}$	$\dfrac{7}{300}$	$\dfrac{23}{11}$	$\dfrac{25}{72}$	$\dfrac{61}{909}$	$\dfrac{11}{18}$	$\dfrac{17}{33}$
	$61.\overline{538461}\%$	$533.\overline{3}\%$	$2.\overline{3}\%$	$209.\overline{09}\%$	$34.72\overline{2}\%$	$6.7\overline{106}\%$	$61.\overline{1}\%$	$51.\overline{51}\%$
Page 39	$\dfrac{5}{11}$	$\dfrac{5}{44}$	$\dfrac{110}{111}$	$\dfrac{100}{9}$	$\dfrac{9}{13}$	$\dfrac{57}{144}$	$\dfrac{65}{33}$	$\dfrac{100}{99}$
	$45.\overline{45}\%$	$11.3\overline{6}\%$	$99.\overline{099}\%$	$1111.\overline{1}\%$	$69.\overline{230769}\%$	$39.583\overline{3}\%$	$196.9\overline{6}\%$	$101.\overline{01}\%$
Page 40	$\dfrac{28}{75}$	$\dfrac{7}{90}$	$\dfrac{300}{11}$	$\dfrac{7}{606}$	$\dfrac{42}{275}$	$\dfrac{808}{999}$	$\dfrac{29}{165}$	$\dfrac{5}{333}$
	$37.\overline{3}\%$	$7.\overline{7}\%$	$2727.\overline{27}\%$	$1.\overline{1551}\%$	$15.\overline{27}\%$	$80.\overline{880}\%$	$17.5\overline{7}\%$	$1.\overline{501}\%$
Page 41	$\dfrac{57}{27}$	$\dfrac{5}{14}$	$\dfrac{16}{15}$	$\dfrac{118}{333}$	$\dfrac{23}{55}$	$\dfrac{43}{22}$	$\dfrac{1}{144}$	$\dfrac{5}{6}$
	$211.\overline{1}\%$	$35.\overline{714285}\%$	$106.\overline{6}\%$	$35.\overline{435}\%$	$41.8\overline{1}\%$	$195.\overline{45}\%$	$0.69\overline{4}\%$	$83.\overline{3}\%$
Page 42	$\dfrac{17}{18}$	$\dfrac{199}{396}$	$\dfrac{19}{27}$	$\dfrac{1}{48}$	$\dfrac{15}{88}$	$\dfrac{35}{36}$	$\dfrac{10}{21}$	$\dfrac{161}{54}$
	$94.\overline{4}\%$	$50.\overline{25}\%$	$70.\overline{370}\%$	$2.08\overline{3}\%$	$17.04\overline{5}\%$	$97.\overline{2}\%$	$47.\overline{619047}\%$	$298.\overline{148}\%$

44

Made in the USA
Lexington, KY
07 May 2012